SARCO the Tasmanian Devil

by

PAULINE REILLY

illustrated by

Kayelene Traynor

We acknowledge with thanks the assistance of Dr Menna Jones who provided additional information for this revised edition.

First published by Kangaroo Press in 1988 as *The Tasmanian Devil* ISBN 0-8641703-4-3.
Reprinted 2001 by Bristlebird Books ISBN 0 9577789 3 7.
This edition revised in 2006 by Bristlebird Books, 1 Manna Gum Close, ANGLESEA 3230, Australia, Tel/Fax 61 03 5263 2011.

Distributed in Australia by INT Press Distribution Tel: 61 3 9326 2416

Printed in Australia by Printgraphics Pty Ltd 03 9562 9600

ISBN 0 9751271 2 8

A wallaby hopped on to the road, then stopped, dazzled by the glaring eyes of a roaring monster.

Too late, the driver of the monster saw the wallaby …

… and drove on, leaving its body on the road.

A mother Tasmanian Devil came out of her den near the road, followed by two of her young.

With growls and yowls and howls, they began to tear off pieces of flesh and bone and fur.

Three other Tasmanian Devils, looking for discarded food at a nearby tourist resort, heard their feasting and fought for a place at the feast. They did not see another car until it stopped with a squealing of brakes, causing all the animals to scatter. When it had passed, the devils returned to their feasting.

But Sarco, one of the devil babies, did not return.

Frightened, she ran off into the darkness. She ran and ran as fast as she could, far away from the road and its fighting devils.

Now, early in the summer, Sarco was alone but she was old enough to look after herself.

Each night, she loped along tracks through the scrub, always searching for food and always ready to hide from people or other scary things.

She ate lizards and large beetles, and tried to catch small furry animals that lived in the bush but they were too quick for her.

Before dawn, she looked for a place to sleep.
Wombat burrows were best if they were empty.

Otherwise, she made a nest of grass under the
shelter of rocks or tussocks.

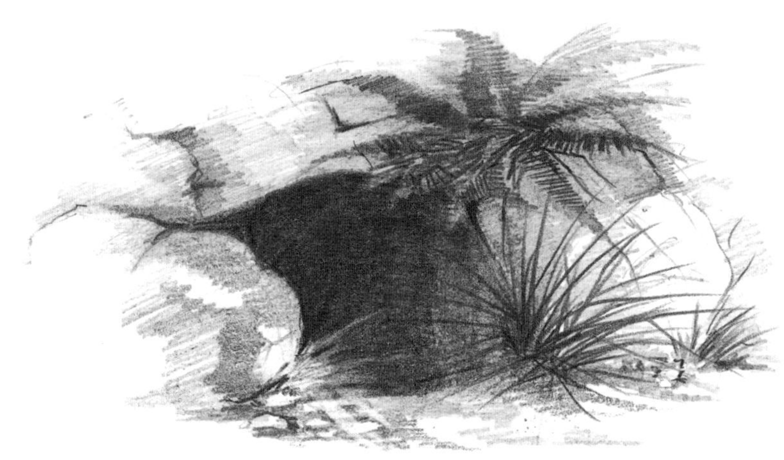

One night she snuffled at the backpack of a sleeping camper. It smelt good. She chewed through the pack, gobbled up a steak and chomped on a chop.

She had just started chewing the camper's smelly socks, when he woke up. He was angry and threw his boots at her. Sarco fled.

On another night, she climbed into a fowl yard and ate a chicken, bones and feathers and all. She returned the next night and the next …

… but this time the chicken farmer was waiting for her. She backed into a corner. She yelped and gaped, showing all her 42 sharp teeth.

The farmer liked devils but he also liked his chickens. He picked up Sarco by the tail, dropped her into a box and closed the lid.

All night long, Sarco whimpered and growled, while she chewed at the box, frantically trying to dig her way out.

Next day, the farmer put the box in his car and drove well away from the farm, down to the seashore. Then he let Sarco go.

Dazzled by sunlight, she fled across the sand and hid under a bush. She heard waves crashing on the shore and smelt the sea.

It was hot and she grew thirsty. At dusk, she crept down to a pool in the sand dunes. She waded into the pool and slurped up the water 'clop, clop, clop' until she was full.

Then she sat and groomed herself. She licked her
front paws to wash her face and head, and
scratched to get rid of ticks and fleas.

She ate dead fish and dead seabirds and sometimes
she ate dead sea-urchins too.

She learnt to catch large moths.

One night, she saw a devil eating a dead wombat.

The devil threatened her but she was too hungry
to run away and began to eat from the other side.
They growled and tugged and pulled and chewed.

Then they fought. They lunged at each other and
crashed their heads together, hissing and
screaming, gasping and gnashing. Sarco won
the fight.

Once, at winter's end, Sarco ran all night looking for food. At daybreak, she was still searching when a dog chased her. She ran and leapt into a river and swam across.

Unaware that the dog had gone home, Sarco kept on running. She climbed up a tree and hid in the branches. Then she heard a twittering and saw a nest full of baby birds. She ate the nestlings, while the angry parents snapped at her head.

In the autumn, Sarco was nearly two years old and ready to mate …

… and so were some male devils. They fought until the strongest male won.

He grasped Sarco's neck with his teeth and dragged her into a burrow. Then, clasping her with his front legs, they mated. He stayed with Sarco for a few days, mating with her often to ensure that he was the father of her babies.

Sarco had to fight to escape from him. Then he went on his way and mated with other females.

About a month later, Sarco gave birth to about 30 babies. Each one, the size of a grain of long-grain rice, slid in a stream of fluid from her birth canal. They crawled into her pouch and the first four fastened their mouths onto its four teats.

The other babies died because they needed a teat of their own to stay alive.

For fifteen weeks the baby devils lived in Sarco's pouch and drank her milk. Each night at dusk, she left them alone in her den but she always returned before dawn.

When she dragged home a dead animal, the babies snuffled and growled while they tore off strips of meat. Sometimes she brought nothing home, but the babies were never hungry because they were still drinking her milk.

They grew bigger, roaming away from the den and learning how to hunt. When they no longer needed their mother, the young devils left her. Those that were still alive when they were two years old, found mates for themselves …

… and so the cycle of life continued.

- Devils live only in Tasmania. They used to live in mainland Australia but died out.

- They are the largest of the flesh-eating marsupials that are known to be still alive.

- Marsupials keep their young in pouches and suckle them.

- Devils are related to the quolls and other small Dasyurids (marsupials that have biting, cutting teeth) and to the Thylacine (Tasmanian Tiger). Thylacines may still live in the wilds of Tasmania but there are no photographs to prove it.

- The scientific name of the Tasmanian Devil is *Sarcophilus laniarius harrisii* (Sar-COFF'-ill-us HAR'-iss-ee- eye). *Sarco* means 'flesh' and *philus* means 'loving'; *laniarius* means 'fitted for tearing'; Harris was the name of the man who first described the devil. It's an animal that tears up flesh, which it likes to eat.

- The devil was given its nasty name because its screams sounded bloodthirsty and people thought it looked ugly and was a killer. It is an efficient hunter and also an efficient scavenger, eating all of its prey except the largest bones. These dead animals would otherwise become smelly and bring flies.

- Devils don't live long lives; perhaps for six or seven years in the wild.

- Feeding food scraps to devils and other wildlife is discouraged as it is considered harmful. Properly controlled Devil restaurants now provide shelters where visitors can watch the devils eating road kills. These educate the watchers to understand the devils' needs.

- To reduce road kills: traffic can be slowed down by speed humps; and the immediate removal of road kills, as well as fences and underpasses, can keep devils off the road.

- In recent years, a disease, that so far is incurable, has attacked and killed most devils once they become adults.

- Tasmania used to be free of foxes but now someone has released a few. Foxes eat baby devils alone in their dens and devils eat baby foxes alone in their dens.

- Many animals eat other animals. Kookaburras eat lizards, seals eat fish, and people eat sheep, cattle, chickens, fish …

Spot-tailed Quoll

Eastern Quoll

Distribution of Tasmanian Devils